inside
boxing

floyd patterson

with
bert randolph sugar

HENRY REGNERY COMPANY • CHICAGO

Library of Congress Cataloging in Publication Data

Patterson, Floyd.
  Inside boxing.

  SUMMARY: Discusses the techniques, exercises,
skills, and strategies of boxing.
  1. Boxing. I. Sugar, Bert Randolph,
joint author. II. Title.
GV1133.P37 1974 796.8'3 74-8266
ISBN 0-8092-8904-0
ISBN 0-8092-8903-2 (pbk.)

Published by Henry Regnery Company, 114 West Illinois Street,
    Chicago, Illinois 60610

Manufactured in the United States of America

Library of Congress Catalog Card Number: 74-6902

International Standard Book Number: 0-8092-8904-0 (cloth)
                                    0-8092-8903-2 (paper)

foreword

Boxing has been practically my whole life for almost as long as I can remember.

I won the world heavyweight championship in 1956, when I was 21. About two and a half years later I lost the title, but in June 1960 I was fortunate enough to regain it.

Boxing has been good to me. Contrary to what you may have heard, not all fighters wind up broke. I was in comfortable circumstances when I took a vacation from boxing late in 1965. I discovered, however, that I missed the challenge of boxing, and I missed the feeling of well-being that comes from being in top physical condition. So I returned to the sport, and today at age 39 I am still an active boxer.

I will continue boxing as long as I can keep giving a good account of myself and feel that I am putting forth my best efforts in the ring.

I have been a professional boxer for more than 20 years. Yet almost every day I still put in several hours of work. In spite of all my experience, I keep learning new things about boxing.

In this book I will try to pass along to you what I've learned, to unlock some of the secrets of the greatest sport in the world. Whether you decide to pursue boxing as an amateur or as a professional, I know that you will enjoy the sport if you will simply follow some of those time-honored and well-founded fundamentals I've learned.

Floyd Patterson

floyd patterson fight record

1951 New York and Eastern Golden Gloves 160-pound Champion
1952 New York, Eastern and Inter-City Golden Gloves 175-pound
    Champion
1952 Olympic Middleweight Champion

1952

Sept.	12	Eddie Godbold, NYC	KO 2
Oct.	6	Sammy Walker, Brooklyn	KO 2
Oct.	21	Lester Jackson, NYC	KO 3
Dec.	29	Lalu Sabotin, Brooklyn	KO 5

1953

Jan.	28	Chester Mieszala, Chicago	KO 5
Apr.	3	Dick Wagner, Brooklyn	W 8
June	1	Gordon Wallace, Brooklyn	KO 3
Oct.	19	Wes Bascom, Brooklyn	W 8
Dec.	14	Dick Wagner, Brooklyn	KO 5

1954

Feb.	15	Yvon Durelle, Brooklyn	W 8
Mar.	30	Sam Brown, Washington	KO 2
Apr.	19	Alvin Williams, Brooklyn	W 8
May	10	Jesse Turner, Brooklyn	W 8
June	7	Joey Maxim, Brooklyn	L 8
July	12	Jacques Royer-Crecy, NYC	KO 7
Aug.	2	Tommy Harrison, Brooklyn	KO 1
Oct.	11	Esau Ferdinand, NYC	W 8
Oct.	22	Joe Gannon, NYC	W 8
Nov.	19	Jimmy Slade, NYC	W 8

1955

Jan.	7	Willie Troy, NYC	KO 5
Jan.	17	Don Grant, Brooklyn	KO 5
Mar.	17	Esau Ferdinand, Oakland	KO 10
June	23	Yvon Durelle, Newcastle	KO 5
July	6	Archie McBride, NYC	KO 7
Sept.	8	Alvin Williams, Moncton	KO 8
Sept.	29	Dave Whitlock, San Francisco	KO 3

Oct. 13 Calvin Brad, Los Angeles   KO   1
Dec.   8 Jimmy Slade, Los Angeles   KO   7

1956

Mar. 12 Jimmy Walls, New Britain   KO   2
Apr. 10 Alvin Williams, Kansas City   KO   3
June   8 Tommy "Hurricane" Jackson, NYC   W 12
Nov. 30 Archie Moore, Chicago   KO   5
      (Won vacant world heavyweight championship)

1957

July 29 Tommy "Hurricane" Jackson, NYC   KO 12
      (Retained world heavyweight champion)
Aug. 22 Pete Rademacher, Seattle   KO   6
      (Retained world heavyweight championship)

1958

Aug. 18 Roy Harris, Los Angeles   KO 12
      (Retained world heavyweight championship)

1959

May   1 Brian London, Indianapolis   KO 11
      (Retained world heavyweight championship)
June 26 Ingemar Johansson, NYC   TKO by 3
      (Lost world heavyweight championship)

1960

June 20 Ingemar Johansson, NYC   KO   5
      (Became first and only man to regain world heavyweight
championship)

1961

Mar. 13 Ingemar Johansson, Miami Beach   KO   6
      (Retained world heavyweight championship)
Dec.   4 Tom McNeeley, Toronto   KO   4
      (Retained world heavyweight championship)

1962

Sept. 25 Sonny Liston, Chicago   TKO by 1
      (Lost world heavyweight championship)

1963

July 22 Sonny Liston, Las Vegas   TKO by 1
      (For world heavyweight championship)

1964

Jan.	6	Sante Amonti, Stockholm	KO 8
July	5	Eddie Machen, Stockholm	W 12
Dec.	12	Charley Powell, San Juan	KO 6

1965

Feb.	1	George Chuvalo, NYC	W 12
May	14	Tod Herring, Stockholm	KO 3
Nov.	22	Cassius Clay, Las Vegas	TKO by 12

(For world heavyweight championship)

1966

Sept.	20	Henry Cooper, London	KO 4

1967

Feb.	13	Willie Johnson, Miami Beach	KO 3
Mar.	30	Bill McMurray, Pittsburgh	KO 1
June	9	Jerry Quarry, Los Angeles	D 10
Oct.	28	Jerry Quarry, Los Angeles	L 12

(Quarter-finals of the heavyweight elimination tournament)

1968

Sept.	14	Jimmy Ellis, Stockholm	L 15

(For NBA heavyweight championship)

1969

(Inactive)

1970

Sept.	15	Charlie Green, NYC	KO 10

1971

Jan.	16	Levi Forte, Miami Beach	KO 2
Mar.	29	Roger Russell, Philadelphia	KO 9
May	26	Terry Daniels, Cleveland	W 10
July	17	Charlie Polite, Erie	W 10
Aug.	21	Vic Brown, Buffalo	W 10
Nov.	23	Charlie Harris, Portland	KO 6

1972

Feb.	11	Oscar Bonavena, NYC	W 10
July	14	Pedro Agosto, NYC	KO 6
Sept.	20	Muhammad Ali, NYC	TKO by 7

Total bouts 64; Won 55, Knockouts 40, Lost 8, Draws 1, TKO'd by 5.

contents

Foreword   1

Floyd Patterson Fight Record   2

1   Before You Begin   7

2   The Basics of Stance and Movement   17

3   Offense   25

4   Defense   41

5   Strategy   49

6   The Workout   55

7   Training and Conditioning   67

    Glossary   74

    Index   77

SUCCESS IN BOXING . . . depends on dedication,
physical conditioning, and long hours spent
in workouts and sparring sessions.

chapter 1
BEFORE YOU BEGIN

At some time in his life, almost every person has clenched his fingers into a fist and used them in self-defense, either seriously or in fun. Fist-fighting is one of the oldest and most universal of human activities. But however instincitive it may be to "put up your dukes" in self-defense, the sport of boxing is not something that can be mastered without study and hard work. You must learn the fundamentals and the more advanced refinements and spend a great deal of time in painstaking practice.

There are many different roads that lead to boxing. For some boxers, interest started with a fight in the streets or the schoolyard. Others began by enrolling in a youth program or going to a gym to get some exercise and seeing some people boxing.

I first got interested in boxing from watching my brothers box, long before I ever climbed the stairs to the Gramercy Gym in New York, where I first began to train. Joe Frazier got interested in boxing after he started going to a gym in an attempt to lose weight. What led George Foreman into the sport was a desire to put his energies to use inside a ring instead of outside one.

But however you get into boxing, you will find it rewarding both as a sport and as an exercise.

WHERE TO LEARN

Almost anyone who wants to learn to box can find a place to do it. Most cities in the United States have Police Athletic Leagues, YMCAs, YMHAs, Boys Clubs, Catholic Youth Organizations, or other groups that sponsor boxing programs. A phone call to one of these organizations or to the sports department of your local newspaper will put you in touch with the right people. In addition, some public schools offer boxing as part of their sports curricula.

If you come from an area where none

of these facilities are available, you will have more difficulty in finding an organized program. If you've bought this book, you still have a good chance of learning to box well. While teaching yourself is not as desirable as having a good trainer, it is a step in the right direction and will help you prepare for the time when you will be able to obtain professional assistance.

RULES

Boxing rules are slightly different for each area of the country, and are interpreted by various governing bodies. However, the rules are almost alike everywhere. You can get a copy of the rules for your area by writing either your local state athletic commission in the state capital (for the professional rules) or your local Amateur Athletic Union office (for the amateur rules).

It's important that you obtain a copy of the rules and become familiar with the small differences that may prevail in your area. But the most important rule to remember is good sportsmanship. It is the foundation of all boxing rules. Boxing rules are intended to make boxing safer and more fair for everyone.

EQUIPMENT

Once you've decided to get serious about boxing, you'll need to become familiar with the proper equipment. Some of the equipment will probably be provided by the gym where you work out, but there are some personal items you'll have to buy for yourself.

The Ring

The ring is the roped enclosure in which the fight takes place. For a professional boxer, it is the most important place in the world—the place where it all happens.

Rings, like boxers, come in all sizes. Some are only 16 feet square, while others are as much as 24 feet square. A 20-foot square is the size most often used.

The ring is surrounded by three or four strands of heavy rope. A canvas covers the floor, and there is always some sort of a mat or cushion under the canvas for safety.

Protective Equipment

Your *protective equipment* includes a *headguard* for *sparring*, a *mouthpiece* to protect your teeth, and a *foulproof cup*.

There are several styles of headguards, which are available with and without *cheek protectors*. I myself don't like the big cheek protectors, but use them if you prefer. Headguards come in small, medium, and large sizes and can be adjusted to fit snugly. Make sure that your headguard is on tight before you start to box; otherwise, the first punch is likely to knock it over your eyes. (One note of caution: when using your headguard in sparring, block high punches by taking them in front of your headguard. Then, in actual competition, you won't tend to rely on the headguard, which isn't there.)

There are quite a few different styles of mouthpieces, ranging from simple, hard-rubber ones that fit anyone and can be purchased in either a drug store or a sporting goods store to the custom-fitted mouthpieces that are made by dentists.

The protective cup is a leather and metal or plastic device that fits around the boxer's waist and shields his hips and groin area from low blows. In an actual fight, the cups are worn under the boxers' trunks. When you're sparring, how-

YOUR PROTECTIVE EQUIPMENT . . . includes a headguard, a mouthpiece
to protect your teeth, and a foulproof cup. Here my brother Ray and
I have donned protective equipment for a sparring session.

CLOTHING FOR BOXING. For fighting, you will need satin trunks as well as a sturdy pair of high-top boxing shoes.

ever, you may want to wear them over your trunks, making it easier to discard them when you're not actually boxing.

Clothing

Another important item of equipment is a pair of high-top leather boxing shoes. You can get along with sneakers when you're just starting out, but by the time you've advanced you should have the real thing.

Boxers wear all sorts of clothing when they're just working out in the gym. You can wear almost any kind of loose-fitting clothing, but you'll find that in the long run it pays to get clothing that's especially made to take the wear and tear of exercising. Various styles of wool training trunks are available—full length, knee length, and regular length (short). If you're hoping to sweat off a few pounds, wear sweat suits and rubber trunks and shirts.

You will also need a robe to ward off the chills that can come when you've worked up a sweat. Terrycloth is best, because it sops up moisture so well. Of course, when you actually start fighting, you may want to invest in a flashy satin robe, if you can afford it.

A ROBE IS NECESSARY . . . for absorbing sweat and warding off chills. For workouts, a terry cloth robe will do fine, but you may want to invest in a satin robe for competition.

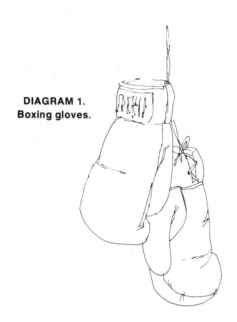

DIAGRAM 1.
Boxing gloves.

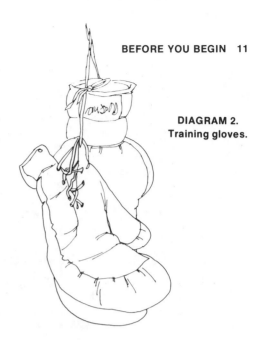

DIAGRAM 2.
Training gloves.

For fighting, you'll need a pair or two of satin trunks. Remember to allow room for your foul protector when you're trying on trunks.

Boxing Gloves

The gloves worn in boxing matches (Diagram 1) are made of leather and are filled with rubber or a synthetic, spongy material. The gloves and their weights are regulated by the local boxing commissions. Amateur gloves usually weigh 12 ounces, although they may weigh up to 14 ounces. Professional boxing gloves vary in weight. Lightweight and middleweight boxers wear 6-ounce gloves, while heavyweight boxers might wear 8-ounce gloves. Many commissions specify 6-ounce gloves, regardless of the weight of the fighters.

The design of the boxing glove has remained the same since 1940. At that time, a bump was added alongside the thumb to prevent the fighter from using the thumb illegally.

Training Equipment

You'll probably have to supply certain items of your own training equipment, although this is not always the case. The boxer usually provides a skip rope, bag gloves, training gloves and, occasionally, a speed bag.

Skip ropes come in either rope or leather. Leather wears longer but it's more expensive, too. You'll need a pair of leather bag gloves for punching the bag, and you also might want a pair of knuckle gloves like the ones I use. These take the place of hand wraps in training. I just slip the big training gloves over the knuckle gloves.

Training gloves, the big overstuffed "pillows" that boxers use in the gym, weigh from 12 to 16 ounces (Diagram 2).

The *speed bag* is a small leather bag that is suspended by a metal swivel from a round platform. The boxer hits the bag very fast. This helps develop coordination and speed. I recommend that you buy a smaller speed bag, called a "peanut" bag. I find that the smaller the bag, the easier it is to hit. I've tried the larger speed bags, but they always throw me off. I can't seem to get any rhythm out of them.

The *heavy bag* is an item of training equipment that is usually provided by the gym. The big bag is made of leather or canvas and is filled with sand. It is

THE SPEED BAG.

used primarily for improving your punching force.

There are many different kinds of "gimmick" punching bags that find favor with different fighters or trainers from time to time. The Europeans, in particular, seem to favor them. For example, some boxers work out with an extry-large heavy bag. There are also weighted bags that stand on the floor and bob around when struck.

José Torres, the former light heavyweight champion, once used an unusually heavy punching bag. It was held upright and supported by heavy wooden beams. The bag was covered with thick layers of foam rubber, which in turn were covered by a mattress cover. The bag was called "Willie" (probably named for Willie Pastrano, the man from whom Torres took the title) and had a human figure drawn on it, with numbers in the vulnerable spots (jaw, stomach, ribs, etc.). A tape recorder was used to bark out numbers from one to eight. "Seven-two-one-four-one-two," it might say, and Torres would then hit the corresponding areas with a left jab, straight right, left hook, right uppercut, left hook, and right cross as quickly as possible. What a novel way to practice combinations.

Torres also liked to use a tiny speed bag for practice in ducking and slipping punches.

And, finally, there was the bag originally used by the old-time trainer Bill Muldoon, who trained Sullivan and Corbett. His was a bag that was anchored by ropes to walls or posts and would duck crazily around. The bag provided excellent target practice for the boxer who was training for a fight with an opponent who moved around a lot.

THE BOXER'S HANDS

The most important tools of a boxer are his hands. And you cannot give too much care to them. Many a promising boxing career has been ruined by broken knuckles or hands. Learning the proper way to protect your hands and knowing how to punch correctly are important in keeping your hands from being injured. More boxers injure their hands in training and sparring than in actual matches.

First, make sure your hands are properly bandaged before you start to work out. Whether you use a training bandage or have your hands bandaged and taped

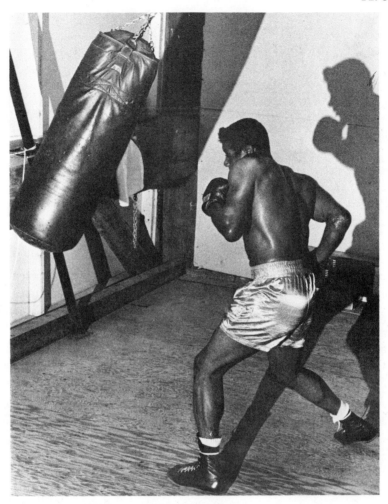

THE HEAVY BAG.

as you would for a fight, be sure that your knuckles and hands are protected and that your fist is solid. If you punch correctly, this will insure you against sprains and breaks.

The old-time fighters often taped their own hands. But nowadays the taping is almost always done by a trainer. If you want to, you could learn how to do it yourself by watching how your trainer does it (Diagram 3).

You might think that the knuckle area is where you would want the most bandages. But it's probably even more important to have the gauze or tape wrapped around your wrist and carried over the back of your hand. The bandage should feel tight or snug when you clench your fist, but not so tight that it cuts off the circulation to the fingers.

Punch only with a tightly closed fist, keeping your knuckles level and up so that the shock of the impact is spread over the entire fist, not concentrated on one spot. Flicking your wrist is dangerous because your hand must be loose for this maneuver, and, as I have said, a loosely held fist is more injury-prone than a tightly held one. Besides, flicking the wrist borders on being an illegal move.

Bone construction can be a factor in hand protection. If your hands are small, with long, thin fingers, they will be more

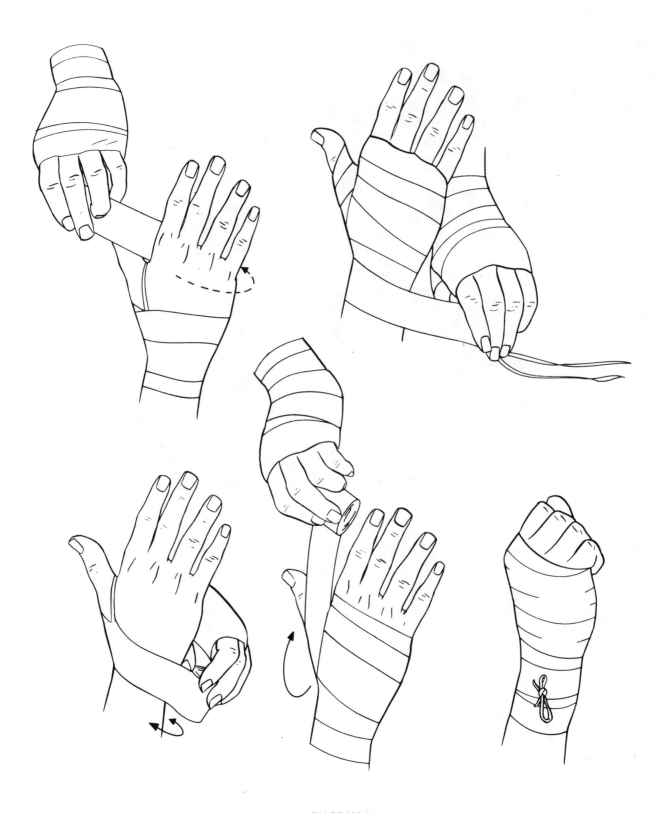

DIAGRAM 3.
Bandaging your own hands.

likely to suffer injuries than if you have a big, heavy hand with thick fingers.

In the old days, fighters used to soak their hands in brine to toughen them, but this really accomplished little. The condition of the skin has nothing to do with the fist. Proper bandaging and proper punching habits are what really count.

If you want to build up your hands and forearms, get yourself a small red rubber ball (sometimes called a "Spaldeen") and squeeze it continually. This can be used not only to build up the muscles of your hand but also to recondition your hands should you injure them.

IN THE BASIC STANCE . . . the feet are properly spaced so as to maintain balance and the hands are held high for both defense and offense.

chapter 2
THE BASICS OF STANCE AND MOVEMENT

Correct stance and movement are the foundation on which to build your offense and defense. Just as a baby learns to crawl before it walks and to walk before it runs, so the beginning boxer must learn the correct stance before learning how to move about the ring, and he must know how to move before concerning himself with punching or with defense.

THE BASIC STANCE

In the basic stance the feet are comfortably apart with the left foot in front of the right and slightly turned in. The distance between your feet should be whatever gives you a solid, balanced feeling; but 12 to 14 inches should be a minimum, so that you cannot be pushed off-balance easily. This position puts you sideways, with the left side· of your body in a straight line with your left leg. This offers a smaller target to your opponent.

Keep your left foot flat on the floor. Your right heel, however, must stay off the floor. Keep your weight evenly distributed between the soles of both feet.

When you back up or move to your right, your right foot moves first, then your left. When you move forward or move to your left, your left foot slides in that direction, followed by your right. Always *slide* forward and backward without crossing your feet. In this manner, you avoid being off balance. If you get off balance, your opponent merely has to shove you to put you on the canvas.

As you move, keep coming back to the basic stance position, the quicker the better. Remember to stay on the toes of your right foot, never placing that foot flat on the canvas. And never bring your feet together or cross them.

Now as to the position of the upper part of your body: keep your left shoulder up and bend your head to the left, so that your chin is hidden in the hollow of your shoulder. It helps, too, if

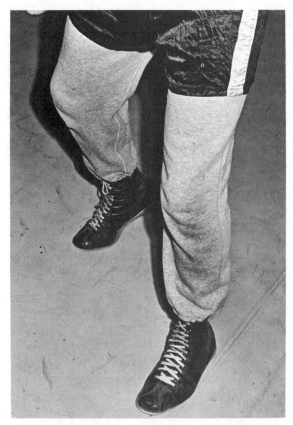

THE POSITION OF THE FEET ... in the basic stance. Your left foot should be flat on the floor and slightly turned in. Your right foot is behind, with the heel off the floor. Reverse these positions if you are left-handed.

tion before your opponent has had time to see your opening and counter your move. An important consideration for any beginner is whether he should stand in the classic position that I've just described or fight out of a crouch. Which position you choose depends upon your particular build and physical attributes. If you are tall and have long arms and legs, your height and reach may enable you to land punches while remaining out of your opponent's reach. Anything you can do to emphasize these advantages will help you. So you'd be better off in the classic stance, with the left side of your body forming a straight line with your left leg and your chin dropped forward and held tight against your breastbone. On the other hand, if you're short, with short arms and legs, then your best

YOUR HEAD POSITION ... offers protection to your jaw and chin, making them poor targets. Here I am showing my pupil how to hold his head properly.

you crouch a bit. This offers protection to your jaw and chin, making them poor targets.

Hold your right hand high and close in beside your chin. Hold your left hand up at all times. Keep your left elbow close to your body to protect your mid-section.

Always come back to this basic position, no matter what you do or where you go. You have to move fast, because whenever you throw a punch you leave yourself open temporarily for a counterpunch. Boxing is a matter of action and interaction. It is impossible to keep from exposing some part of yourself from time to time. So you must learn to be fast in returning to your basic defensive posi-

bet would be to make yourself into a smaller target by crouching. You'll find that you can explode out of a crouch in an effective offense. And, on defense, you will be harder to hit.

If you have an average build—neither very tall nor very short—I'd advise you to learn both methods of fighting, because the situation may arise when you'll need to change your stance against opponents with varying builds and fighting styles.

Keep your body relaxed. If you tighten up, you'll get tired, but if you keep your body limber, you'll be able to do a lot more. The only time you should tighten up is when your opponent is throwing punches at you. When you're throwing punches or moving, try to be as limber as possible.

FIGHTING OUT OF A CROUCH ... is an effective method for a fighter who is short or of average height. The crouch makes your body a smaller target, and exploding out of the crouch is an effective offense.

MAINTAIN THE BASIC STANCE ... even while moving around. Here I'm showing my pupil how to slide forward without losing his balance.

When you're first getting started, it's a good idea to pay a great deal of attention to your footwork, so that it becomes second nature to you. Unless you work on your footwork, you'll probably get tangled up when you try to move around in an actual fight. First practice moving in and out; then try to move from side to side. Then try to speed up your changing movements without getting off on the wrong foot.

BOBBING AND WEAVING

Footwork is not the only type of movement you must learn. As a beginner you also need to master *bobbing and weaving,* the side-to-side and up-and-down movement of the body that is useful on

DIAGRAM 4.
Bobbing and weaving.

SPLIT-SECOND TIMING . . . is necessary if you are to avoid the punches being thrown at you. Bobbing and weaving makes you harder to hit because you're a moving target.

both defense and offense (Diagram 4). Bobbing and weaving is the art of slipping and sliding punches. It is also called "ducking" or "avoiding."

After fighting for awhile, you may decide that this way of fighting is not for you. But even the boxers who prefer to fight in the classic stand-up manner find that, sometimes, a bit of bobbing and weaving comes in handy. I think it's important for every beginner to learn this technique.

When you're bobbing and weaving, keep your eyes on your opponent at all times. Some fighters look their opponents in the eye; others watch the chest; still others look at their opponent's feet. I find that by looking at my opponent's chest I can tell everything that's going on. But I know that the other methods work better for other fighters.

SLIPPING A PUNCH . . . is an important technique for every beginner to learn.

BOBBING AND WEAVING . . . is primarily a defensive measure, but it can also be used offensively. To offset the longer reach of your opponent, you can punch out of a weave, as I'm preparing to do here.

Whatever target you train for, keep your eyes glued on that spot, the place where you know what's going on. This takes plenty of practice. Many times I've gotten in trouble because I took my eyes off my opponent's chest and looked at the floor instead. So I keep working, training myself to watch the chest, to make sure that I'm never caught by surprise in an actual fight.

You can practice bobbing and weaving in front of a mirror or by ducking the swinging, heavy bag or a smaller bag. The smaller bag that I use is made to go from side to side or forwards and backwards, and is perfect for bobbing and weaving practice.

It takes split-second timing to avoid punches being thrown at you. And just as important as making your opponent miss is being able to be in a position yourself to counterattack. Always be a moving target. Shift your feet, go in and out, move sideways. Move your upper body, too, as well as your head and shoulders. Movement is your best defense when your opponent gets through your guard.

Practice moving your head and shoulders without moving the rest of your body. Bend your knees and rock on your toes. Go into a deep crouch and move all over the ring. Move around smoothly without jumping or jerking.

Bobbing and weaving can be an effective offensive manuever, too. It allows you to escape your opponent's blows and still remain in range for a counterattack. For example, you can drop your body forward from the waist so that your opponent's punches pass harmlessly over your head. Carrying your hands high, with elbows down, you are ready in such a case to come right back with your own countering punches. Punching out of a weave can give you added leverage as you swat from side to side.

THE JAB . . . is the basic offensive weapon in boxing. The classic style of jabbing is straight from the shoulder.

chapter 3
OFFENSE

Every boxer has his own distinctive style of offense, but all boxers depend on a few basic punches—the *jab,* the *right hook,* the *left hook,* the *uppercut,* and the *right cross.* If you master these punches, you can use them to devise your own style and strategy of fighting.

THE JAB

The jab is the first punch most beginners learn. It is your basic weapon in boxing (Diagram 5). The jab is far from the simple movement it appears to be. Its proper execution requires perfect timing and balance.

The jab is important not only because it is a fine offensive weapon, throwing your opponent off balance and creating openings for other punches, but also because it is a crucial defensive weapon. It can be used effectively in blocking your opponent's right cross.

The jab proved to be a deadly weapon for Ingemar Johansson. It was Johans-son's left jab that set Eddie Machen up for the right-hand punch that knocked Machen out in the first round. And, in 1959, when Ingemar knocked me out to gain the heavyweight crown, it was his left jab that did it. In the actual fight, his left jab didn't hurt at all. He caught me many times with it, but it was not proving to be an effective nor a devastating punch—or so I thought. After a while, I decided to stop wasting my energies in knocking down his left jab. Instead, I decided that I would just avoid the jab and think in terms of going on the offensive. It didn't occur to me that his left jab was merely setting me up for his right hand. Johansson TKO'd me that night in three rounds. And I would credit the TKO not to the right-hand punch he landed but to his left jab, which had set me up for the punch.

In a later chapter, I will talk about the right jab, the offensive weapon for left-handed fighters. If you are right-handed,

DIAGRAM 5.
The jab.

SHOULDER AND ARM POSITIONS . . . are crucial in getting force behind your jab. As I'm showing my student in these pictures, the arm should be kept straight but relaxed, and the fist should be turned at the moment of impact.

here's how to throw the *left* jab properly. Make a quarter turn of your body to the right and extend your left arm. Start with the laces of your glove turned in toward you. Extend your arm, not too stiffly or tensely. Rotate your fist at the moment of impact, turning your hand over so that the laces now face down. Hit with the flat of your knuckles, so that you won't risk injury to your wrist.

The classic style of jabbing is straight from the shoulder, using an extended, forward motion of the arm. Follow your straight left arm and step toward your opponent, moving your left foot. Step forward on your right foot and lift your right heel to maintain balance. Keep

your thumb in, not only when you jab, but when you throw any punch. Keep your hands high so that your head and body are protected.

Move fast and bring the left hand back to the basic position quickly after you throw the jab. Practice continually so that you can jab and return in a flash. Each time you jab, bring your fist back just far enough to get leverage, then stick your arm out again. (You'll hear some of the more advanced trainers yelling to their fighters: "Stick it, stick it." By this, they mean "Jab.") When you jab quickly and repeatedly, you are setting your opponent up for what is to follow, your right cross, your left hook, or whatever other punch you might throw.

The classic approach works well for most fighters, but every boxer should adopt a style that is natural for him. Many great fighters have thrown their jabs from other positions, often starting with their left hands down at the waist or even dangling at their sides. There is no one correct way of doing anything. However, in order to improvise and find your own style, you must begin with the basics and go from there. There are no shortcuts. By not knowing the basic movements, you will only penalize yourself and have little to fall back on.

A jab should be thrown at eye level, but if you are short and and will be facing men taller than yourself, you will have to jab upward. By the same token, if you are taller, you will have to jab with a downward motion. If you are taller than your opponents, you will find the jab an especially fine weapon to have in your arsenal. While a jab is generally used only to the head, it can be effectively employed against the body if you are facing a taller opponent who holds his hands high.

Practice makes perfect, and this is especially true of the jab. There are many ways that you can work to develop your jab. The heavy bag is the best method. Away from the gym, having a friend or your trainer hold up the palms of his hands for you to jab at will help sharpen up your jab. This method is excellent, as your partner can move around, moving his hands up, down, side-to-side, and in other directions, thus providing an unpredictable moving target.

THE RIGHT HOOK

The right hook is a short, punishing blow that produces tremendous power be-

USING YOUR PARTNER'S PALM AS A TARGET . . . is a good way to practice the jab, especially if he moves his hand around to give you a shifting target.

cause it has the entire weight of the boxer's body behind it (Diagram 6). While purists insist that only a "southpaw" can deliver a right hook, a right-handed boxer can also throw this punch. Deliver this punch as you would a straight right jab, but bend your elbow away and raise your body up about 5 inches. As your fist hits your opponent, the laces of your gloves should be facing in instead of down.

Archie Moore and Sandy Saddler, two great former champions and two of George Foreman's trainers, always advocated that the boxer turn his weight into the punch as he threw it. Maybe this is why they scored 140 and 103 knockouts during their careers, respectively. Throwing your weight before the punch reduces the effectiveness of the punch. Use your weight to follow through, in a

DIAGRAM 6.
The right hook.

manner similar to driving a baseball after you've hit it with the bat. The right hook, which is very effective when delivered in close to the body, should be delivered with the weight shifting from the right foot to the left foot.

THE LEFT HOOK
When delivered properly, the left hook is the most devastating punch in boxing (Diagram 7).

It takes a lot of practice to deliver this punch with power, but it is well worth it.

Starting from the basic stance position, lean slightly forward and to the left, placing your weight on your left foot. Keeping your left elbow and arm in close to your body, turn your left hip and shoulder to the right. Keep your fist turned inward, laces inside and thumb up. Step forward, shifting your weight from your right foot to your left as you throw or whip the punch, raising your elbow about 4 inches. The left hook should be delivered in either an upward

DIAGRAM 7.
The left hook.

THE LEFT HOOK . . . depends on proper balance, speed, and coordination. Here I'm working with my student to correct his stance. Practice the movements of the left hook until they are spontaneous.

or level swing, depending on whether you are delivering the punch to the head or the body.

This punch can be delivered equally well from in close or at a distance. When you deliver it from a distance, however, remember to take a sliding forward step as you swing. I cannot overemphasize the need to *shift your weight as you deliver the punch to gain maximum impact.*

I myself like to deliver the left hook from a half crouch. When I leap forward I add the leg spring to the muscle power and weight behind the punch. I used this version of the left hook to bring back the heavyweight title when I knocked out Ingemar Johansson in five rounds in the Polo Grounds in 1960.

To practice the left hook, use the heavy bag and sparring with others. Shadow boxing and working out in front of a mirror will also help.

THE UPPERCUT

The uppercut is most effective for *in-fighting* because it doesn't require much room to deliver. Throw the punch in an upward motion, with your laces facing you, so that the full force of your knuckles makes contact with your opponent's chin (Diagram 8).

The uppercut is delivered in the same manner whether you use the left or the right hand. Bend your knees forward slightly, putting all of your weight behind the blow as you step in, swinging your arm upward. Your weight shifts to your left foot for a left uppercut and to your right foot for a right uppercut. This helps the fighter maintain his balance and get the maximum amount of weight and power behind each punch.

Like any punch, the uppercut takes a lot of practice to perfect, and it is one that few fighters master. But it can be

DIAGRAM 8.
The uppercut.

PUT ALL YOUR WEIGHT . . . behind the blow when delivering the uppercut.

DIAGRAM 9.
The right cross.

important to you in a fight that is fought in close quarters.

THE RIGHT CROSS

The left jab and the right cross form the classic one-two, the perfect combination in boxing. The jab opens the offensive and the right cross closes it.

Deliver the right cross from the classic stance. Hit right from the shoulder, with all of your weight behind the punch. As you release the punch, give your body a quick twist or turn at the waist, putting your weight on the ball of your right foot. Raise your elbow so that your arm is almost straight. As your arm crosses over from the right to the left side, your glove should be turned so that the laces are down (Diagram 9).

Your right leg should move forward as you step in with your left, and your weight should shift directly over to your straight left leg. In this manner, as you turn your hip and shoulder to the left, you will be able to deliver a sharp, stunning blow to your opponent's head.

Maintain the proper balance and hold your left hand close to your body in a guarding position so that you are not left open to a counterpunch by your opponent.

INFIGHTING

Infighting—fighting at close range—is an important aspect of boxing. In many ways it has become, like its main weapon, body punching, a lost art. Too many of today's fighters are content merely to grab and hold when they get in close, clinching and waiting for the referee to break them apart rather than fighting in close. And, too often, they don't even clinch correctly.

Infighting usually has been a short man's game. Short arms are best suited for infighting and a short body makes for a smaller target, easier to defend. For some shorter men, like Rocky Marciano, infighting became a necessary tactic.

Position is the prime ingredient in infighting. The basic body, foot, arm and hand positions are the same for offense and defense in effective infighting. You need to maintain good balance, with your weight properly set, your knees slightly bent, your body bent at the waist, and your hand's held in close,

with your arms protecting your sides. This position lets you be on the offensive one moment and on the defensive the next.

Bobbing and weaving is an effective tactic for the infighter. You can duck in close to your opponent and come up punching. Short punches, hooks to the head and to the body, uppercuts and straight, short digs to the body are the tools of the good infighter.

Use your weight to press against your rival. The secret of good infighting is to keep your opponent off balance. Keep your hands inside your opponent's arms, so that while you're able to deliver your punches, your arms act as defensive blocks for the punches he throws at you. A good infighter learns to attack and to counter, taking every opportunity to turn the tide in his favor.

Although hitting and holding is an illegal practice, tying up both of your rival's arms and hands while keeping one of yours free is not only perfectly legal, but smart boxing. This is not an easy maneuver, but one that can be a big plus for you. Draw your opponent's arms together in front of him and wrap or pin your own arm around them from underneath. A competent referee will allow a man who has pinned his opponent's arms and has one free hand to punch with his free hand. Bringing your head or shoulder up underneath the chin of your rival is also an illegal move, but using your shoulder to press an opponent off balance is not.

Training for infighting is a grind, but it is necessary. There are, of course, natural athletes in boxing as in other sports, but they are few, and most of us must depend on devotion and hard work to make the grade. I feel that lack of discipline is one of the reasons there are so

INFIGHTING . . . is the art of fighting at close range. It is one of the best weapons of the average or short boxer. The secret of good infighting is to keep your opponent off balance.

FEINTING ... can be used to draw punches from your opponent.

few accomplished infighters today. If you want to succeed as a fighter you must be able to continue your fight on the inside. Infighting is much harder to learn and master than standing at long range and boxing. For those who master it, infighting can turn the tide in a close bout.

FEINTING

Like infighting and body punching, feinting has become a lost art. It is merely the art of out-thinking your rival and putting your ideas into practice.

José Torres, my former stablemate and the light heavyweight champion of the world, wrote a book called *Sting Like*

FIGHTING OUT OF A CROUCH ... is a good offensive weapon for someone who can move fast and has proper balance. From my well-known "Peek-a-boo" defense, I can explode with a straight right to my opponent's head.

a Bee. In his book, he gives the best definition of a feint I've ever heard: "A feint is an outright lie. You make believe you're going to hit your opponent in one place, he covers the spot and your punch lands on the other side. A left hook off the jab is a classy lie. You're converting an I into an L. Making openings is starting a conversation with a guy, so another guy (your other hand) can come and hit him with a baseball bat."

Remember, the hand is quicker than the eye. Being able to get your opponent to look for one thing, and then doing another is feinting. Feinting is using your head to draw an opponent into committing himself and then taking advantage of that commitment to counter him. Feinting is pretending to go to the body so your opponent drops his guard, and then going to his head, or vice versa. It is looking one place and punching another, or moving your feet as if to throw a left, when you're really going to throw a right.

All of these methods of feinting can be perfected, but only through long, hard hours of practice. Again, a mirror is the place to start; then progress into sparring sessions. Don't be disgusted with yourself if you fail at first—just keep practicing. The ability to out-think your opponent is essential to being a top-flight or championship-caliber boxer.

FIGHTING OUT OF A CROUCH

Like infighting, fighting out of a crouch works best for a short boxer. It makes him an even smaller target. But if you can't develop a good style of infighting, don't try fighting out of a crouch. A taller, long-armed opponent will just stay out of range and jab until you make a mistake—then BAM.

Bobbing and weaving is important to someone who fights out of a crouch, as is infighting. Another consideration is balance. If you don't have proper balance, just a slight jab to the shoulder or to the top of your head could push you off balance, leaving you wide open.

Archie Moore and James J. Jeffries were two big men who fought out of a crouch. I often fight out of a semi-crouch, to which my own "peek-a-boo" style is best suited.

When you fight out of a crouch, you must also be able to punch fast. Henry Armstrong and Joe Frazier are two boxers who throw their punches in bunches. Quick flurries are important to a crouch fighter, as he doesn't have the style to set up his rival with probing jabs as does the straight, stand-up boxer.

PICKING OFF PUNCHES . . . requires quick reflexes. When properly done, it gives the fighter a psychological and strategic edge over his opponent.

chapter 4
DEFENSE

Defensive moves are the tactics a boxer uses to avoid getting hit solidly. These include such moves as *blocking* or *slipping* punches, moving out of range, or moving inside the arc of a punch. It is important to learn the proper defensive moves. No matter how hard a hitter you are, or how strong, you will one day come up against someone who will be able to handle your punches and who may hurt you. That's when you must apply your knowledge of defense and defensive tactics. Even the unbeaten Rocky Marciano was knocked down twice, though he got up to beat both men —Walcott and Moore.

When a punch is thrown at you, you have a choice of several different ways of avoiding it. You can block the punch with your hand, arm, elbow, or shoulder. Or you can pick it off with your glove, sometimes called *parrying*. Another choice is to *go with the punch,* moving your head in the direction of the punch.

SLIPPING PUNCHES

The big advantage to slipping or ducking a punch instead of blocking or parrying it is that you still have both of your hands free, ready to counterpunch.

The proper way to slip a punch is to move to the inside line. In other words, to avoid a right punch, move your head to the right, and to slip a left, move your head to the left (Diagram 10). This leaves you in the perfect position to counterpunch. If you move to the outside—that is, to the left when your opponent throws a right or to the right when your opponent throws a left—your opponent's arm will be blocking you. He may even have hit you as you moved into his punch.

Bobbing and weaving is an effective technique in slipping punches, one that I like because it allows me to come up swinging. Learning to punch from a bob and weave takes practice, but the defensive and offensive advantages it gives

DIAGRAM 10.
Slipping a punch.

you make it well worth the effort. When bobbing and weaving, alter your moves. If you keep making the same moves over and over, it won't take your opponent long to figure you out. When bobbing and weaving, I always watch my opponent's chest. By doing so I can tell what punches he is going to throw. I can also tell approximately where his head is so that I can go on the offensive quickly and land my own punches. I try to slip beneath a right or a left or a combination of punches to get in close and initiate infighting.

BLOCKING, PICKING OFF, SLIPPING, AND DUCKING PUNCHES . . . are the most important defensive moves. Use your arms as well as your hands in blocking. All of these moves depend on quickness and proper balance.

DIAGRAM 11.
Blocking a hook.

When you first start boxing, you may find that you instinctively pull your head back when you see a punch coming. This can be very dangerous. The only fighter I've ever seen who gets away with this is Cassius Clay (Muhammed Ali). But, unless you have great speed, you'll get into trouble by pulling back, because it upsets your balance.

Another reaction to avoid is moving straight back when your opponent charges in. It is much more effective, and just as easy, to move to the side, getting off a counterpunch at the same time.

BLOCKING PUNCHES

Blocking or picking off a jab, or parry-ing, can be done in either one of two ways, depending on the type of jab being thrown at you. If the jab comes straight from your opponent's shoulder, extend your left arm sideways from the proper stance position, just enough to knock or brush the blow to the outside. If your opponent is jabbing from a lower guard position, you can either catch the jab in the open palm of your right glove or press downward with your right, knocking the blow down and away from you.

In blocking a hook, keep your elbows in tight next to your body. Hold your arms slightly in front of you so that if the blow is to your head you can just raise

DIAGRAM 12.
Blocking a punch thrown at the body.

your arm slightly, and if the blow is aimed at your body you can absorb the force of the punch on your arm by bending your body just a little (Diagram 11).

When blocking any punch thrown at the body—whether it be a left hook, a right uppercut, or a straight right jab—always use only one arm to block the punch. If your opponent throws a left hook to your body, use your right elbow to block it. If he throws a straight right, use either your right or your left elbow to block it. If you use both arms to block a punch, you'll leave your ribs wide open (Diagram 12).

To block a right cross or a straight

right, use your left arm in an outward motion, pushing the punch away from your body. This technique is used to counter the classic jab. No matter what punch your opponent throws, try to block it by forcing his arm to the outside, leaving you in the best position to counter.

There are all kinds of variations on defense. My so-called *peek-a-boo* style is one of them. I keep both hands level, holding them a few inches in front of and to the side of my head. This allows me to use my gloves to block punches thrown at my head and to use my elbows to block body punches.

Archie Moore used to fold his arms

MY "PEEK-A-BOO" DEFENSE . . . allows me to use my gloves to block punches thrown at my head and my elbows to block punches thrown at my body.

with his elbows pointing out across his body. He hid behind his arms in what he called his "Armadillo" defense. Each of you will discover what's best for you after a while. But first, learn the "book" method so that you have a base from which to improvise.

COUNTERPUNCHING

Sometimes the best defense is a good offense. Counterpunching is the way you go onto the offensive from being on the defensive. Remember, any time your opponent throws a punch, he creates an opening for you. Counterpunching is the art of exploiting these openings and turning them to your advantage.

Let's say that your opponent is throwing a left jab at your face. What are your options? One—you could block his left jab with your right glove and throw a jab, either taking his jab or deflecting it to the outside in a swatting motion with your own left. Two—if you are just sizing up your opponent early in a fight, you might just want to slip the punch to the side or simply move out of range. This will allow you to see if he brings his left back to the proper position or leaves it low after he punches. If he leaves it low you can come over it with your own right the next time he jabs. Slipping the punch also gives you the chance to see how fast or slow his punches are.

Nobody can keep from getting tagged forever, no matter how fast and clever and elusive he is. Years ago, people used to talk about what a great defensive boxer Willie Pep was. And believe me, he was really great. They used to say that it was practically impossible to hit Willie anywhere but on the seat of his pants. But if you take a good look at Willie today, you'll know he stopped a few punches with his face. There is no such thing as a perfect defense.

THE CLINCH

Suppose your efforts to avoid punches have been unsuccessful. You're on the defensive, all right, but you're catching your opponent's leather. What do you do in that case? Desperate situations call for desperate solutions. Try to tie your opponent up in a *clinch*. Clinching means holding your opponent's arms so that he cannot strike a blow. By moving in on your opponent and pinning both of his arms to your body with your arms entwining them on the outside, you can gain additional time after missing a blow. Gaining time can be especially crucial when you're hurt or tired. I don't normally advise boxers to hold, and I don't use this tactic much myself, but you should know about it as a method for getting a breather and as part of your defensive makeup.

In the final analysis, defense is a matter of instinctive self-preservation. It is up to you to sharpen your instincts by knowing all of the fundamentals of defensive boxing.

A SMART BOXER . . . is one who makes the best use of all his physical attributes.

chapter 5
STRATEGY

Although you should throw the basic punches in a consistent, correct way, you must adapt them to fit your own particular needs. Obviously, if you are a 5 foot, 2 inch welterweight you won't fight in the same style as you would if you were a 6 footer. Short boxers should become aggressive infighters, body punchers, and bobbers and weavers. If you are tall and lanky with long arms, then boxing, as opposed to slugging, should be your "thing." Making use of your physical attributes is smart. You must deploy all the weapons at your command.

Speed is what separates the superstars from the stars. If you possess speed of hand for quick punching ability or speed of foot for swift boxing skill, then you have a great natural advantage. Use it wisely; don't try to be a slugger if you have speed. Sluggers develop their style because they lack other skills. If you find that you have a heavy punch, develop it,

but remember that it is not necessary to take one to land one. It is far better to make your opponent miss and counterpunch him.

THE INTANGIBLES

There are three important intangible elements that must be discussed in a chapter on boxing strategy: When to "throw away the book," when to break training, and how to use fear to your advantage.

When To "Throw Away the Book."

Whenever you feel like it, you must throw away the book and throw *combinations*. A combination can be far more devastating than any single punch, and you must be prepared to improvise.

A boxer is allowed to throw any type of punch he chooses, as long as he throws it properly and with great speed. In my younger days, when I was fighting in the Eastern Parkway Arena over in

Brooklyn, I would sometimes throw four or five right hands in a row, followed by three left hooks and then a right uppercut to the body. If you look at some of the films of my early fights, you'll see what I mean. This combination was unheard of, but it worked for me because I practiced it over and over again.

Another example of successful improvising, is the *"Gazelle Punch,"* which I originated, as far as I know. I would leap in the air to hit an opponent. This punch stopped an awful lot of people. I used it against Archie Moore in 1956 when I first won the heavyweight championship as well as against Ingemar Johansson when I regained the title in 1960.

Kid Gavilan's "bolo punch" is another example of what can happen when a fighter throws away the book and creates something that works for him.

The question to ask in improvising a punch is, "Does it work?" You won't know until you try. Try a new combination early and try it often. If it doesn't work, discard it.

When To Break Training

One rule that should never be violated is to break training camp or take a break from training at least two or three days before a fight. This simple rule is mighty important. The only thing that is as bad for you as undertraining for a fight is overtraining for it.

I'm talking from my own experience. In 1959, before my first fight with Ingemar Johansson, I didn't understand that when a fighter trains for long periods of time, building his body into the peak of condition, he needs a two- or three-day break right before the fight to be at his maximum physical and mental strength at the fight itself. I boxed just

two days before my fight with Ingemar, and I did roadwork the day before the fight. He broke camp a full seven days before the fight. I couldn't understand why at the time. But with experience I came to understand it. Your body is already in top physical form after your long period, even months, of training. In the days before a fight, you must build yourself up mentally. Don't worry about getting out of condition by taking a few days off before a fight. When you're in top physical condition, you don't get out of condition that quickly.

In the days right before the fight, I may take a walk, but that's all. No boxing, no roadwork. I find that after a day or two, my body wants to fight. All the energy I put into training starts coming back to me. And both my mind and my body are at their peak on the day of the fight.

Fear and How To Use It To Your Advantage

I suppose there are some fighters who don't know the meaning of fear, who never feel nervous before a fight. But I don't personally know any boxers who don't get "butterflies" in their stomachs before a fight. And, as far as I'm concerned, that's good, because fear can work for you. You don't have to be afraid of fear.

Let me tell you how fear worked for me. Back in my amateur days—I think it was my third fight—I had to fight a fellow named Julius Griffin. He was a heavyweight, a very big, muscular guy. At that time I was only 15 years old and I weighed only about 157 pounds. But they needed an extra bout at the Downtown Athletic Club in New York, and I had been begging my trainer, then Frank Lavelle, to get me a fight, any fight. So he agreed to let me fight Griffin.

When I saw that big, muscular boxer, I didn't want to fight him. But I didn't want to back down because that would have made me look like a coward. So I went ahead with it. But, believe me, I was scared. I couldn't even look at him when I entered the ring. I remember that I didn't have a robe, just a towel around my neck. The referee gave us instructions, but I have no idea what he said, because at that point my body and mind were numb with fear. I went back to the corner, they pulled the towel off me, and the bell rang.

I remember turning around and seeing this big monster-giant coming at me, all muscles. I don't remember what happened afterward. The next thing I remember is the referee telling me something about a "neutral corner." I didn't quite understand what had happened. I looked down, and there was Griffin on the floor. I had knocked him out. I couldn't believe it.

It wasn't until I got back to the dressing room that I found out what had happened. I didn't want to ask anyone, so I just sort of felt my way through it, saying something like, "Gee, he caught me with a good punch." And then someone told me that Griffin had come directly at me and had backed me into a corner. I had jumped up in the air with that "Gazelle Punch," and hit him about ten times before my feet hit the ground. As he was going down, I had followed him down, throwing punches all the way. The referee had to pull me off of him. That is what fear did for me.

If you're still not convinced that fear can help a fighter, consider the antics of Cassius Clay (Muhammad Ali) before his first fight with Sonny Liston. Clay bragged, ranted, and raved at the weigh-in so much that the commission head had him fined $2,500. But he managed to work on Liston's fear. Clay's manager, Angelo Dundee, had said: "With that kind of fear, I'd face a cage of lions. Man, Cassius will win." And win he did.

I always tell fighters that it's a good thing to be nervous when you go into the ring. When you're nervous, you know that you'll use all you've got and take advantage of every opportunity. Nervousness makes you sharper. When you understand this you won't worry about being afraid.

Of course, it doesn't work that way with all fighters. I've seen some boxers drained of everything they had by fear, looking around for a place that was comfortable to sort of fall down in. But, with most fighters, a little fear along with nervousness never hurts. It even goes a long way.

THE SOUTHPAW

If you happen to be one of those lucky people who were born left-handed, and if you are smart enough not to allow yourself to be switched from this superior stance when you take up boxing, you will enjoy a distinct advantage in the ring.

For some reason it has always been thought of as more difficult to box a southpaw than a right-handed boxer. Some countries and promoters even go so far as to forbid the unorthodox stance of a left-hander. If you are a southpaw, the most difficult thing for you to do is to box another left-hander, for southpaws usually make a career out of boxing right-handed fighters and giving them "fits."

Most left-handed boxers fight from a semi-squared stance, with their right leg only slightly in front of the left. For this

THE LEFT-HANDED BOXER . . . must learn the same proper stance as the right-handed boxer, except that the feet and arm positions are reversed. If you're left-handed, lead with your right foot and use your left foot for balance and leverage.

reason, a right jab is not one of the better offensive weapons of the southpaw. The right hook, the left cross, and the left uppercut are the prime weapons of attack for a southpaw. By moving to his left, the left-hander can confuse a right-hander even while he is moving into the power hand of his rival.

There is no real reason why a left-hander cannot be a stand-up boxer. However, the southpaw is usually taught by a right-hander and is not shown how to use his right jab properly. But the right jab, like any other punch can be developed with long hours of practice on a heavy bag, by shadow boxing, or by sparring.

While there are many southpaws in the amateur ranks, most boxers get "turned around" when they become professionals. Among the most successful southpaws are former heavyweight champion George Foreman and Carmen Basilio, the man who won both the welterweight and middleweight championships. I myself have fought only one southpaw in my entire professional career.

If you're left-handed, be sure to exploit the fact that your opponent tends to be somewhat confused by fighting a southpaw.

Fighting Against the Southpaw

One of the strongest myths in boxing is that the way to beat a left-hander is by throwing right hands. This is simply not true. A left hook is the most effective weapon against a southpaw. As noted before, most southpaws fight from an almost closed or square stance. Few are good jabbers, so that their right is either thrown as a hook or in a pawing jab. This makes it easier to beat them to the punch with a left hook than by throwing right hands. An orthodox or right-handed fighter shooting straight rights at the head of a southpaw is leaving himself wide open for countering lefts to the body, and, in throwing his right, he is stepping into the power hand of the southpaw. This is something that doesn't happen when he attacks with his left hook, for few southpaws have any sort of power in their right hands.

But whether you are fighting a left- or a right-handed fighter, it is most important that you fight your own fight. Don't try to alter your style to offset your opponent's style, because then you are fighting his fight, not yours.

SHADOW BOXING . . . in front of a mirror improves
timing, coordination, and hand and foot speed.

chapter 6
THE WORKOUT

A boxer's workouts begin and end with exercises. Before the vigorous work in the ring, it is necessary to be warmed up and loosened up. To get the kinks out, go through a systematic "shake-down cruise" of all the parts of your body.

Start from the top down, rolling your head and neck around, first in one direction, then the other. Then shrug your shoulders and rotate them. Next, bend at the waist, forward, backward, and sideways, touching your toes, bending your knees, whirling your arms in their shoulder sockets, jumping and bouncing around, and doing a little light shadow boxing. By this time you should be pretty well loosened up.

SHADOW BOXING

Few people outside the world of boxing seem to understand the importance of shadow boxing. Most spectators are under the impression that it is a kind of loosening-up exercise. Actually, shadow boxing is an extremely important form of training, which benefits both the fighter's mind and body. In fact, it is so important that professional boxers often practice shadow boxing only moments before they go into combat.

Usually in your workout you are hitting something—the speed bag, the heavy bag, or an opponent. But in shadow boxing, all you're hitting is air. In an actual fight, you'll find there are many times that you miss your opponent and hit nothing. When you do this, you can hurt your arm by pulling a muscle if you don't know how to throw a punch, miss, and pull your arm back correctly.

Another function of shadow boxing is that it allows you to practice and perfect various moves and combinations of punches. Because your opponent is imaginary, you can relax and concentrate entirely on throwing the sequence of three or four or five punches in the correct manner while simultaneously executing your footwork properly. For example, to counter an imaginary opponent's lead, your trainer may want you to step back and then fire a right hand over the imaginary left jab, bending in as you punch.

In order to be effective, these movements must be coordinated smoothly. Before you can try them out on an actual opponent—whether in the ring or in the sparring session—you should be able to do them by yourself. As you shadow box, the moves gradually become automatic and instinctive. In shadow boxing, you quickly learn that your body must be relaxed. If you are tense, your movements will be slower. Strive for relaxation of tension, for speed, and for smoothness.

Practice set patterns—don't throw punches aimlessly. Otherwise, you'll learn in a haphazard manner. Throw two jabs, a left hook and a right cross. Throw a hook to the body and a hook to the head—left-right-left. Develop a pattern for each series of punches.

Most gyms have full-length mirrors that you can use in shadow boxing. This enables you to watch your own movements, to see what your opponent will eventually see. You can shadow box without a mirror. But always keep your imaginary opponent in mind as you move around and continue to practice your combinations.

Shadow boxing should be done in three-minute rounds, with the standard one-minute rest in between. Include two rounds of shadow boxing in every workout.

SPARRING

To each fighter, sparring represents something different. If you're a beginning fighter, it is a joy, a release after so many long hours of the dull work of learning and practicing at the gym, exercising, shadow boxing, and working on the bags. It is a chance to get into a ring and hit and be hit, the opportunity to test yourself against something other than inanimate objects and your own shadow. Sparring is an opportunity for the beginner with a lust for combat to earn a split lip or a black eye—badges of courage for the aspiring pugilist. It is also a chance for the novice to build up his confidence under "real" battle conditions.

As you progress and do more sparring, it is the chance to learn, sometimes painfully, of your mistakes. It is the classroom where the lessons you learned in the gym are put to use. It is where you must hone and correct your tools, for your sparring mate is also learning. When you miss or drop your hands, he is learning see your error and take advantage of it. So sparring becomes less play and more work as you move up the ladder.

It has always been my belief that, until a fighter has become a pro, he is better off sparring with fighters who are in a better class than himself. In this way he can learn from them. There is nothing like a sparring session to uncover your mistakes. And it is much better to find your errors and correct them in a sparring session than in a real fight, when it may be too late to do anything.

In the sparring ring, the strategy that you and your trainer plotted in the gym and in the corner is first carried out. It is also in the sparring ring that you learn your strong points as well as your weak ones. Your showing in the sparring ring tells you and your trainer what all those weeks of working out have taught you.

Sparring also gives you some "on-the-job" training to further your career in the ring.

PUNCHING THE BAG

No workout is ever complete without punching the bag. Bag-punching usually follows the workout with your sparring partners. While there are many varieties of punching bags, they fall, basically, into two categories: the light bag, or speed bag, and the heavy bag.

SPARRING . . . gives you "on the job training" for actual competition.

HITTING THE SPEED BAG ... may take you some time to learn, but it is the best way to develop speed, hand-eye coordination, and arm strength.

The Light Bag

The basic purpose of working out with the light bag is to develop speed of hand. The speed bag also sharpens your hand-eye coordination and strengthens your shoulder and arm muscles, in addition to helping you punch faster.

It took me quite a while to learn how to hit the speed bag. In fact, I didn't really learn how to do it until I was 20 years old—and I won the heavyweight championship when I was 21. Because I didn't know how to hit the speed bag, I would stay away from it. It looked too complicated to try and I didn't want to fail in the presence of all the other people in the gym. But after a while, I began to go to the gym before anyone else and practice hitting the speed bag. I practiced it very, very, slowly. Eventually, after weeks of practice, I was hitting it faster. I don't really know how long it

took me to master the technique of hitting the speed bag in a rat-a-tat-tat fashion, but it was a long time. So don't get discouraged if the technique doesn't seem to come to you right away.

In order for you to hit it correctly, the bag must be at the correct height. When the bag is at rest, the bottom of it should be about level with your eyes. Wear light leather "bag gloves" when punching the speed bag.

You can develop many different bag-punching routines, but, in the beginning, stick to the standard practice of striking the bag twice in a row with the same hand. Stand before the bag with your fists up, your elbows forward and raised so that your upper arm is parallel with the floor. Stand far enough away from the bag so that it will not strike your head when it rebounds from your blows.

Strike first with the front of your knuckles, then with the back of the same hand, then with the knuckles of the other hand, and then the back of it. In order to keep the bag moving back and forth, it is necessary to keep hitting it rhythmically. If you break the rhythm, the bag will bob around crazily. When this happens, allow the bag to come to rest and then resume your punching. Never try to hit a bag that has started to bob around. You could strike the swivel and hurt your hand.

Eventually you will develop your own rhythm in hitting the speed bag, and you will find that you are developing a rhythm in your legs as well as in your hands. In addition, you'll find that when you're hitting the bag with your right hand, you'll be sort of pivoting or stepping up and down with your right leg. This becomes automatic after awhile.

To break the monotony of the bag drill, try to catch the moving bag with an occasional hard punch. (Caution: Make sure that you don't crack your knuckles on the swivel. More than one fighter has

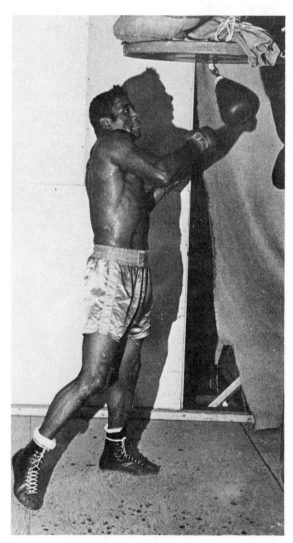

PRACTICE QUICK PUNCHES . . . on the speed bag to get experience in moving fast on the offensive. Eventually you will develop your own rhythm, in your legs as well as your hands.

HITTING THE HEAVY BAG . . . helps to strengthen the muscles in your shoulders and legs as well as to improve your punching power.

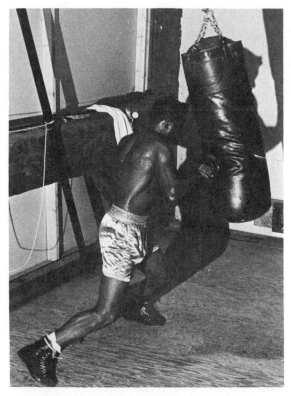

PRACTICE YOUR SOLID PUNCHES . . . on the heavy bag to develop power. Here I'm practicing a left hook to the body and a right jab.

suffered broken bones in his hand from just this kind of accident.)

The Heavy Bag

Just as the purpose of the light bag is speed, so the purpose of the heavy bag is power. The big bag is primarily used for developing and improving punching force and leverage.

The heavy bag can be used hanging free or held by a trainer, to give you extra leverage. Either way, it represents an opponent—except that it doesn't hit back.

In a workout with a free-swinging heavy bag, you also get practice in using your weight to maneuver an opponent. Shove the bag away, and, as it swings back to you, throw one or two punches. Shove it away again, bob or duck out of the way as it comes at you, then when it swings back again, throw one or two hard punches.

The more the bag moves, the more you will move. If you've worked out with a bag that moves very little, you'll tend to move very little when you're boxing. If you get a bag that swings way out and goes all the way around you (the kind I have), you'll find that you'll have to move quite a bit more to catch up with it.

I try to throw four, five, or six combination punches at the heavy bag. The same combinations that I throw at a heavy bag during training are the ones I'll throw during an actual fight. Most fighters use the heavy bag as an opponent. George Foreman used the heavy bag almost exclusively in preparing for his title fight against Joe Frazier, shoving it aside and hitting it hard in the area where Joe's ribs would be. He followed almost the exact pattern during the fight, with some measure of success.

You can use the heavy bag in a defensive drill by bobbing under it and to the side as it comes toward you. A good flexibility drill is to duck completely under it, crouching low to the floor. But watch out that it doesn't hit you when it is swinging back. This care will teach you to watch out that your opponent doesn't hit you with a second punch after you have ducked the first.

SKIPPING ROPE

Rope-skipping is part of your regular workout routine, after your sparring and bag punching. Rope-skipping helps develop footwork, coordination of feet and hands, and general flexibility of arms, wrists, and legs.

Like your other training activities, rope-skipping should be controlled by the clock. Skip rope for at least two or three rounds each session, a round being 3 minutes long.

I try to make at least 150 jumps a minute, which means that in 3 minutes I've done 450 jumps. At times I've been able to jump 525 or 550 times in 3 minutes. Counting the jumps gives you something to think about while you're jumping and helps you jump faster. Faster jumping gives you a lot more stamina and makes your legs move even faster.

When I'm jumping I often move around. I do this purposely to try to make both legs work together as they have to when I'm fighting. I also try different steps. Instead of the straight-up-and-down jump, I try to jump heel-to-toe or execute double jumps just to mix my legs up. This lets me know that my legs are working together and can come back

together in a correct stance and not in an awkward position.

Some boxers have trouble jumping rope. They always seem to be tangled up. If you can't get the hang of it at first, you might try just jumping alongside of the rope, spinning it with one hand and imitating the rhythm of a real rope going over your head while you jump for your three minutes. You could vary it by changing hands. Every now and then, try really jumping the rope. Sooner or later you'll be able to do it.

When I first started I couldn't jump rope and would purposely stay away from any rope-skipping exercises when any of the other fighters were around because I was embarrassed to be seen stumbling over the rope. I eventually learned by standing on the edge of the ring, about 5 or 6 inches above the floor, and jumping down to the floor as the rope passed under my feet. I would then jump back onto the raised surface and prepare to jump off of it and over the rope the next time it came over my head. In this manner, I learned to jump rope and found it to be an invaluable training aid for balance and foot coordination.

Some boxers I know like to have some music playing in the background while they jump rope. It takes their minds off of what they're doing. Sonny Liston always used to have a record of "Night Train" playing. I'll bet he wore out a dozen copies of that record during his workouts.

FLOORWORK

The calisthenics that wind up each training session are known as *floorwork,* because that's exactly where you do most of them. The purpose of these exercises is to strengthen the muscles that come into play in a boxing match.

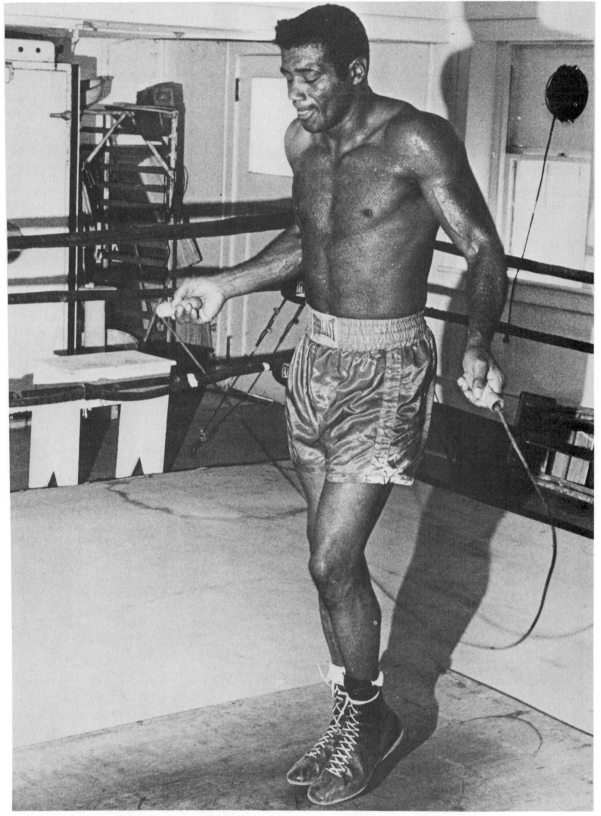

SKIPPING ROPE . . . is good for your wind, your shoulder and arm strength, and your footwork.

One of the most important of the floor exercises is *sit-ups*, which strengthen the abdominal muscles. I like to use a slant board for sit-ups, putting my feet higher than my head. I find that this creates more tension and strengthens my muscles more. Sit-ups should be done at a fairly rapid pace. You can do them in either one of two ways—with your hands clenched behind your head, touching your elbow to your knee, or with your hands outstretched, touching the tips of your fingers to your toes. I prefer the first method. As I come up to a sitting position, I pivot at the waist and bring my right elbow to my left knee, or vice versa. This twisting body motion also brings the side muscles into play and strengthens them.

The best exercise to strengthen the neck muscles is *bridging*. Lie on your stomach on a mat and push halfway up. Put your forehead down onto the padding and then gradually shift your support from your arms to your head. With your weight entirely supported by your toes and your head, fall slightly to either side. Then let yourself down to the mat, roll onto your back, and force yourself up in the air with your weight on the back of your head and your feet. Again, shift your weight slightly to either side.

There's no better exercise to help build up your shoulder muscles than

SIT-UPS . . . are a good exercise. They strengthen your stomach muscles and increase your endurance. Doing them on a slant board creates more tension and builds up muscles more.

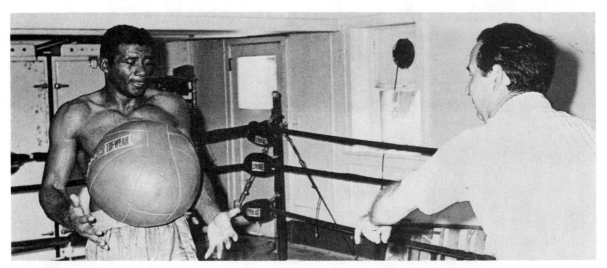

THE MEDICINE BALL . . . is a hard rubber ball used to harden the muscles of the torso. Have your trainer throw the ball at your stomach, as you see me doing here, or put the ball on the floor and roll on top of it.

push-ups. You can make them tougher still by putting your weight on your fingertips rather than on the flat of your hands. Another variation on the traditional push-up is an exercise called *the dipper.* Starting from a standing position, go into a crouch, with your hands touching the floor. Then extend your legs backwards, full length. Your weight is now on your hands and feet. Then dip your body down to the floor, push up until your arms are fully extended again, and bring your legs back under you. Then stand up straight.

You can also get a good workout if you work with the *medicine ball.* The best way to use it is just to engage in a game of "catch" with a partner or with your trainer, catching the ball in your stomach. Some boxers prefer merely to roll around on top of the ball, hardening their muscles in that manner.

After a strenuous workout, many fighters have massages and rubdowns. Done by trainers who know what they're doing, these can help take the soreness and stiffness out of your muscles. I also find a whirlpool bath to be a big help after a long workout.

Incidentally, even though I had suggested that you could use any kind of loose-fitting clothing, I strongly recommend a loose-fitting flannel gym suit for a workout. The gym suit absorbs perspiration and tends to keep the body free from irritation, while fitting comfortably.

The man who tends to be heavy must work a bit harder than one who is thin and should wear heavier clothes when he works out. If you're overweight, watch your diet very closely. Weight classifications in boxing are very rigid, and sometimes you can eat yourself out of a division in which you would have succeeded. (As a warning to those who think that moving up a division is child's play, remember Archie Moore's observation: "Heavyweights' jabs feel like light-heavyweights' knockout punches.")

ROADWORK . . . is boring sometimes, but I know how important it is to my conditioning. Regular running has been proved to strengthen your heart, improve your wind, increase your endurance, and give you more energy.

chapter 7
TRAINING AND CONDITIONING

To me, training is one of the most enjoyable parts of boxing. The feeling that you get from having a well-conditioned body and mind makes the hard work, time, and sweat you've invested worthwhile. In fact, because you're in shape, you enjoy the hard work that may follow.

Let's face it: You cannot be a good boxer unless you are in good condition. You may know all the fancy moves in the world, and you may possess the most devastating punch. But if you lack the stamina that comes from physical and mental conditioning, chances are you'll never get very far. Proper training is the cornerstone upon which champions are built. Notice that I said *proper* training. Haphazard methods are bound to fail.

Training is not something you can do when you're in the mood and skip when you feel lazy or your friends have some activity lined up that sounds a lot more interesting. Training is a day-in, day-out affair, a routine. It must become a way of life to you if you want to be a boxer.

Your trainer should be a person who has boxed or who knows boxing. Having a trainer who cannot box or who does not know boxing is like having a secretary who can't type.

Before you start a regular program of training, it makes good sense to get a medical checkup. Professional boxers get them regularly. Boxing is a vigorous, strenuous sport that makes great physical demands on your body. Your doctor or your hospital clinic can quickly check your heart and blood pressure as well as your overall general health.

Chances are that if you're planning to do some boxing, you're already a fairly athletic sort of person. Quite possibly you figure that you don't really need much in the way of exercises to get yourself into condition to box a few 2-minute rounds. You couldn't be more wrong! If you've ever watched a couple of sub-novice Golden Glove boxers huffing and puffing after only a minute of action, laughed at their comical swings and misses, and noticed them slowing down even more to gulp down some oxygen, you'll realize that what I'm telling you is true.

Of course, there are some very rare people blessed with such splendid physiques and in such excellent condition before they come to boxing that they can take it all in stride. But, believe me, most of us poor mortals have to work, and work hard.

Your first important objectives are to harden your body and improve your wind. Honest training should make a man thoroughly sound and fit; no other kind of boxer should enter the ring.

MUSCLE DEVELOPMENT

If you're a young boxer seeking to build yourself up for the rigors of a very demanding sport, you will find my recommendations on exercise in the previous chapter very helpful. In addition, there are other things you can do to build up the specific muscles that come into play in boxing. Both weight training and isometrics may be helpful.

Weight Training for Strength

Muscles are developed by working them close to their limits. In weight training for strength, you take a different approach from the one you must take when lifting weights for endurance. In training to build up your strength, use heavier weights and fewer repetitions. Any weight lifting program should be carefully supervised by someone who is a qualified instructor.

Weights for Endurance

Weight training in boxing takes two forms. First there is body building for the young, beginning boxer. Another type of weight training builds strength and endurance. Weight training in boxing is somewhat controversial. Some trainers swear by it, while others swear at it. Generally speaking, few mature or experienced boxers use weights. I am opposed to weightlifting by boxers, because it makes the muscles too tight, especially in the arms. The more flexible and limber you are, the faster you can deliver your punches.

While it is undoubtedly true that regular workouts with weights can increase both strength and endurance, there is some concern about this type of training adversely affecting a boxer's hand speed. If weight training is to be used as a part of your training program, it is very important that a graduated program be set up—starting with very light weights and progressing slowly to heavier ones.

The most useful exercises are the dumbbell press, curl, wrist curl, and deltoid exercise (arms extended, lifted sideways). All of these benefit arms, shoulders, and wrists. Use lightweight dumbbells, with many repetitions of the movements. Your goal is endurance, so the exercises should be repeated rapidly, in ever increasing numbers.

Doing sit-ups with weights behind your neck or on your chest will benefit your stomach muscles, while squats with weights will develop your thighs. Weighted boots can be used for leg and abdominal exercises.

In using weights to develop endurance (as opposed to strength), I must stress again the cardinal rule: Don't try to lift too much. Weight training is merely a supplement to your regular exercise program, and should not be considered a substitute for it.

Isometrics

Isometrics is another excellent way of developing strength. The principle of isometrics is to use one muscle or group of muscles full strength for approximately 6 seconds. Experts have found that isometric exercises achieve maximum muscle development more rapidly than conventional exercises, which, because they require many repetitions, take much longer.

Isometrics is based on the idea of the immovable object pitted against an irresistible force. If you clasp your hands together and then try with all of your might to wrench them apart, or press one hand against the other as hard as you can, you are doing isometrics.

Lock your hands behind your head and push backward as hard as possible with your head, and you have an isometric exercise for the neck muscles. Put your hands on your forehead and press or push upwards or sidewards on a door jamb, or take an unbendable steel rod and try to bend it or twist it—these are all isometric exercises and all help develop your muscles. Make sure, however, that you keep up the pressure for a full 6 seconds.

These isometric exercises will build up the strength of your muscles. But they will not help your stamina, wind, or endurance at all. For that you need floorwork, roadwork, and other exercises.

ROADWORK

The best single conditioner is roadwork —simple running. Not only does running benefit your legs, but it works wonders on the rest of your muscles, too, especially your heart, which is actually a mass of muscles, and your lungs. Jogging has become the "in" thing for execu-

tives who want to stay in shape, ever since the benefits of running have become known.

Roadwork is the simpliest kind of exercise of all to do. You just get out and run. All you need in the way of equipment is clothing that is suited to the weather and that is not too tight or binding, plus properly fitted sneakers or shoes.

Where to run? If you live in the country or in the suburbs, that's no problem. In the city, you can usually find a public park or a school track. It is best to keep away from busy streets, with their fumes and smoke from traffic, and all of their noise and distractions.

In the beginning, don't overdo the roadwork. Run a half-mile or a mile, alternately walking and jogging, depending on your physical condition when you start. Skip a day and then repeat the same procedure. Do this for a week or ten days, gradually building up your distance. Don't try to break any speed records. Remember, you're not training for a track meet. You want to box.

After a while, you will find that you are running faster, farther, and more easily. You'll also find you have a new spring to your step and more energy than you can recall having had in the past. There will probably be times, as you're running, when you'll feel the impulse to sprint for a short distance. Do it. Then, go back to your easy stride.

Even after you become an advanced boxer, you must continue to run. You never outgrow the need for roadwork. But, while you must do it faithfully, it is important not to overdo it.

Billy Graham, the fine welterweight of a few years back, told a story that illustrates my point. It seems that Charlie Fusari, who was a ranking welterweight in his day, came up to the training camp in Greenwood Lake, New York, to train for a bout with Sugar Ray Robinson. Fusari was unfamiliar with the camp, so he asked Graham, who had trained there frequently, "Where do you run?" "Around the lake," said Billy, not actually meaning completely around the lake, which was quite large, but along the shore for a mile and a half or so, then reversing the procedure and running back.

But Fusari took him literally, and, as Graham tells it, ran all the way around the lake, something on the order of an Olympic marathon run. "He was in bed for three days," recalls Graham, who added that Robinson beat Fusari over 15 tough rounds.

The amount of roadwork you do depends upon several factors: the number of rounds you're preparing to fight; the importance of the fight; your need to get up or down to a specified weight; and the individual needs of your own body.

If you're preparing for a three-round amateur bout, it stands to reason that you will not have to make the same demands on your body that you would if you were about to engage in a 15-round championship contest.

Just as the factors dictating the need for roadwork vary, so does the routine for roadwork. Many boxers like to run 3 or 4 miles every day for two weeks before a fight. Others, myself included, prefer to run three or four times a week even when they're not preparing for an immediate fight. That way you're always in condition.

Most boxers like to do their running early in the morning. The advantage, particularly in the big cities, is that the air is cleaner and there isn't as much noise or congestion on your route.

I prefer living and training in the country, where there's plenty of fresh air, trees, and quiet. But it really doesn't matter what your surroundings are. The important thing is that you just get out there and run.

Sometimes it's very difficult to make yourself get up early in the morning and get out and run. Let's face it, all of us get lazy at times. And at those times you're likely to make excuses for yourself. It's happened to me a couple of times. I've gotten up in the morning with absolutely no desire to do roadwork, and said to myself, "Well, I ran two or three miles yesterday and I trained hard in the gym. Maybe I'm pushing too hard. I don't want to overtrain. Maybe I should take the day off."

Well, I was just kidding myself. It wasn't true that I had overtrained. I just had to force myself to get up, put on my roadwork clothes, and get out there.

There is one way I can tell if I've really overtrained. It's when I feel tight and my muscles ache. That's the first sign. When that happens, I just go back to bed. Some days I don't even go to the gym, because to overtrain can be worse than not being in condition at all. Never overpush your body.

There is one other important rule to remember. When you return to your quarters after running, strip in a room free of drafts and take a warm shower or bath to loosen your muscles. Then, after the shower, make a complete change of clothing to keep from catching a cold.

Like everything else, roadwork can become boring. I like to think of things to make it more interesting. Believe it or not, sometimes I even count my steps and see how far I can go in a thousand steps. Or sometimes I run backwards to see if I can run a thousand steps back-

A WELL-CONDITIONED ATHLETE... enjoys many sports. I find skiing a great way to stay in shape and help my balance and timing.

wards. At other times I see if I can run a mile in a certain amount of time, or see how long it takes me to go two or three miles. I always try to beat my own record. Things like this make the running more interesting. Sometimes I count things—such as rocks or tin cans or license plates—just to keep my mind occupied.

Remember, a good pair of legs is one of the most important assets of a boxer. Walking and running a lot are essential for your success in the ring. Your legs are the first things to give out when you're out of condition. I can't overemphasize the importance of roadwork. It is the first step toward becoming a boxer.

GOOD HEALTH RULES

As long as you feel well, you probably don't give too much thought to your body. But if you're a boxer, your body is too important for you to take it for granted. If you follow a few simple rules

you'll find that you'll stay generally healthy.

Get plenty of sleep. That's the time when the body repairs itself and gets rid of the poisons that accumulate. You'll find that you weigh less after a good night's sleep and, curiously, are a bit taller in the morning, too. In addition to sleep, your body needs some relaxation from the strain and tension of your daily activities.

Personal cleanliness is also important, not only because it discourages germs but also because you cannot afford to become sick. Oddly enough, I've noticed that boxers who are in prime physical condition are often quite susceptible to colds. If you shower after a workout in the gym, make sure you don't run right out into the cold. Avoid drafts and chills if you can. When you shower, wear shower shoes to avoid athlete's foot.

I take at least two or three whirlpool baths a week when I'm in active training, to keep my circulation going and my body loose. If I feel stiff or tense, the whirlpool bath will loosen me up.

In addition to the medical check-ups, which all boxers must undergo, you should also take care of your teeth. Visit your dentist at least twice a year, and follow his instructions for keeping your teeth and gums healthy. While I'm on the subject of teeth—make sure you have a good-fitting mouthpiece. If you have one of the inexpensive store-bought types, ask your dentist or your trainer if it's doing the correct job for you.

It almost goes without saying that a boxer should not smoke, drink alcoholic beverages, or use drugs. You can't afford to abuse your body, for it is your workshop and if it is damaged, so is your potential career.

Good health rules are largely a matter of using common sense. Most of us know what's good for us and what's not. The rest is will power.

DIET

There's a well-known saying: "You are what you eat." A boxer must always keep that in mind. You can't expect to eat a lot of junk and not feel the effects. Eat a well-balanced diet, with emphasis on proteins. Most fighters eat only two meals a day, breakfast and dinner, when they're engaged in full-time training. Others, especially those who divide their time between training and a full-time job, find that they prefer three meals a day, with a light lunch.

Whatever your schedule of meals, you can't eat too soon before or after any kind of workout, whether it's in the gym or on the road. The fighter who does his running early in the morning usually is ready for breakfast around 10:00 A.M. Breakfast should include some cereal,

eggs (boiled or poached, but not fried), toast, and tea with lemon.

Dinner should be a substantial meal. In a fight camp, it comes at about 6:00 P.M. The main course should be some kind of lean meat, (steak, lamb chops, or chicken), fresh vegetables, a baked potato, salad, and fresh or canned fruit for dessert. The beverage, again, should be tea.

Almost all boxers drink tea, not only because its warmth relaxes them, but also because it contains much less caffeine than either coffee and soft drinks. Tea tends to work on the body more quickly than coffee to cleanse it of impurities. (By tea, I mean warm or hot tea, not iced tea.)

If you eat lunch, it should be a light meal, possibly just toast and tea with a little bit of fruit.

A fighter's diet, of course, must sometimes be varied according to his individual needs. Fighters who must watch their weight must be careful of what they eat. But they must be even more careful of the amount of fluid they drink.

"Drying out," or restricting the intake of liquids, is a common practice for a day or two prior to an important fight. It is done for the purpose of sharpening up and speeding up the reflexes. However, it should not be undertaken without the supervision of an experienced trainer.

Even when I'm not in training for a specific fight, I watch what I eat. I try to stay away from all fried foods. My foods are always boiled, baked, or broiled. I also take vitamin pills to supplement my diet. When you're training or doing roadwork, you burn up an awful lot of energy, and must tailor your diet so that you eat the right foods that provide you with extra energy. I always eat a lot of fresh fruits and drink a lot of tea to replace the fluid that I lose in a workout. Finally, I stay away from pastry, because it gives me indigestion—and, of course, I don't touch tobacco.

MENTAL ATTITUDE

Just as important as your physical conditioning is the development of your mental attitude. You must have the right outlook, the right frame of mind, and the right approach to boxing. A good mental outlook is, of course, easier to achieve if you have done all of your homework in the gym and are in top physical condition. Physical and mental conditioning go hand in hand. When you know that you are in top condition, it makes your mental attitude that much better. You become confident of your ability. There is no nagging feeling that you have cheated, because the only one you can really cheat is yourself. You may let down your manager, your trainer, your family, and your friends; but if you are not in the prime of condition, the only one who will suffer is you.

When you find that you have mastered the fundamentals of boxing and that you are expert enough not to get hit, you will gain additional confidence. Knowing that you are not going to get hit as often is one of the most important qualities that a fighter can learn. When you sense that you are not going to get hit as often, then two very important intellectual processes are being exercised: the sense of anticipation and the sense of confidence. Not getting hit as often improves one's own desire; confidence builds up the will; desire, confidence, and will all build up your intelligence—your ability to think fast and to coordinate your body movements.

If you're in good mental shape, you not only have the will to win, but you are also properly conditioned to accept defeat. If you give your best, then you can accept defeat, knowing that you were beaten by a man who was better than you—at that moment. Making alibis and offering excuses are signs of not having the proper mental outlook. After all, no one is unbeatable. Learning to accept defeat as well as victory—and coming back after defeat to win once again—are the best signs of a fighter who has the proper mental attitude.

PUTTING IT ALL TOGETHER

Knowing how to deliver all the punches, knowing the rules, mastering the methods of defense, knowing the moves and the countermoves, are all the pieces of a jigsaw puzzle. Putting these pieces together is a must for a successful boxer.

Again, I have to stress the importance of devotion, diligence, and desire to train and practice. You will spend many long hours in the gym, training, sparring, and working out, without seeming to be making any progress. Then one day it will happen. You will have put it all together and the feeling of satisfaction will be well worth the effort, the hard work, and the long hours.

If you're thinking about making a career in boxing, you have to do some real soul searching. You must ask yourself if it's really what you want. If it is, then you must tell yourself: "I must give my whole self to the sport, not just part of me."

You must have a certain kind of determination to do this, because the hardest thing of all is not the training, but the sacrificing. In the end, you will find that all the training and all the sacrificing have brought you the happiness that goes with success. I know, because I took that road.

glossary

Apron: The part of the ring floor that extends beyond the ropes.

Art of Hitting: The science of obtaining maximum power in punching with the minimum of effort.

Attack: Successful leads or blows struck first—not counterpunches.

Back: 1. To retreat from an opponent, though facing him. 2. The rear part of the anatomy from the neck to the waist. Deliberate blows to the back are allowed.

Backhand Punch: A foul blow landed with the back of the glove.

Backpedal: To retreat from an opponent though still facing him.

Backward Shuffle: To retreat slowly with both feet on the floor at all times, maintaining balance for both attack and defense.

Balance: Proper holding of the body and coordination of the limbs during a contest.

Bandages: The hand covering used by boxers, which consists of soft cotton or linen and not more than one layer of soft adhesive tape for fastening to the wrist. One roll of 2-inch cotton gauze or linen bandage, not to exceed 10 yards in length, may be used for each hand.

Barrage: A succession of fast and hard punches by one boxer against another.

Beat to the Punch: To hit the opponent first, although his punch was started at the same time, or even before.

Bell: The gong that is used to signal the start and finish of a round.

Belt. 1. The line around the body at a level of the navel. 2. To hit an opponent hard and often.

Between Rounds: The interval of one minute duration, from the end of one round to the beginning of the next.

Blocking: Picking off an opponent's punch with the glove, arms, elbows, or shoulder.

Blow: A punch landed with the fist.

Bobbing and Weaving: A swaying, side-to-side and up and down movement of the body, usually from a slight crouch, used in an attempt to present a moving, more difficult, target to the opponent.

Body Punch: A punch aimed to the opponent's body.

Boxer: A fighter who brings cool judgment, calculation, ring generalship, fine point of tactics, and scientific thought to aid his punching, as opposed to the slugger.

Break: The order by the referee to both the boxers to disengage from a clinch. On this command, each boxer must take one step back before continuing to box.

Butt: To hit the opponent with head or shoulder. This is a major foul.

Button: The point of the chin.

Clinching: Locking arms by both opponents when they get close to each other.

Counterpunch: A punch thrown after the opponent leads.

Coverup: A defensive maneuver in which the crook of the right arm protects the head and the left arm covers the body.

Cross: A counter blow that crosses over the opponent's lead.

Crouch: A position in which the body is bent low with the head forward. The crouch can be used both as an offensive and defensive position.

Crowd: To move in close to your opponent, not giving him punching room.

Drop: To knock down an opponent.

Ducking: Dropping the upper portion of the body forward to get under hooks and swings thrown to the head. A method of avoiding blows and staying in counterpunching range.

Dukes: The fists.

Elbowing: The use of the elbows to press against the face or throat of your opponent. A foul.

Fancy Dan: A clever, light-hitting boxer who takes no chances by fighting only defensively.

Feint: A false lead to one part of the body of your opponent, used to draw him off guard.

Flick: To strike a blow with an open glove. This is an illegal move.

Floor: To knock an opponent down.

Foul: An infraction of the rules.

Heavy Bag: A large canvas- or leather-covered bag filled with sand, sawdust, or other material, which is used to develop punching power.

Heeling: Hitting with the inside of the glove or butt of the hand. A foul.

Holding: Locking or gripping an opponent's arm or glove.

Hook: A punch delivered at close range from the side, with the elbow swinging out and hooked.

Infighting: Fighting at close range.

Jab: A straight punch delivered by a right-hander to the head or body. The lead blow in a one-two combination.

Kayo: The knockout—shortened to K.O.

Kidney Punch: A blow that lands at the back over the kidney. When thrown in close, it is a foul.

Knockdown: The flooring of an opponent.

Knockout: A situation in which one boxer has been floored and is unable to get up within 10 seconds. *See also* Technical Knockout.

Low Blow: A blow below the belt line.

Make Use of the Ring: To use evasive tactics against an opponent by moving about the ring.

Mouthpiece: A rubber or plastic protector used as a covering for the teeth.

Neutral Corner: The two corners of the ring not used by the fighters between rounds.

Outbox: To box distinctly better than an opponent.

Outpoint: To gain the decision of the officials over your opponent.

Rabbit Punch: A sharp blow delivered to the back of the head or neck. A foul.

Reach: The distance from the tip of the middle finger of one hand to the other.

Right Cross: A right hook; a right-hand punch that crosses from right to left.

Right to the Jaw: A punch delivered at short range straight from the shoulder to the jaw.

Right Uppercut: A rapid rising blow with the right hand.

Rolling: Moving the body with the opponent's punch. Against a straight blow, the movement is backward; against hooks, to either side, and against uppercuts, the body movement is backward and away.

Shadow Boxing: Practice at sparring and hitting against a nonexistent opponent.

Slipping: To avoid a punch by moving the head or body away from the punch, to either side.

Slugfest: A match in which there is heavy hitting, with little or no defense.

Sparring Partner: A person who spars or boxes with a fighter during training.

Spoiler: A fighter who never makes it to the top, but in most cases manages to make a good fighter look bad. Such a boxer does win occasionally, but always when least expected.

Stand-up Boxer: A person who fights from the orthodox stance.

Straight Left: A punch designed to keep an opponent off balance. It is delivered straight from the shoulder. Also called a left jab.

Straight Right: A punch like the straight left, except it is delivered with the right hand. When used by a left-handed boxer it is called a right jab.

Technical Knockout (TKO): A situation in which a fight is stopped by the referee due to an injury, or when the fight is stopped to prevent the beaten boxer from taking too much punishment.

Tie up: To clinch, to lock the arms of your opponent so as to prevent him from throwing punches.

Uppercut: A blow delivered with the arm bent, straightening out as the body is stretched or straightened.

index

Agosto, Pedro, 4
Ali, Muhammad, 4, 44, 51
Amonti, Sante, 3
Armstrong, Henry, 39

Bandaging hands, 12-15
Bascom, Wes, 2
Basic Stance, 17-19
Basilio, Carmen, 53
Blocking punches, 44-47
Bobbing and weaving, 19-23, 41
Bonavena, Oscar, 4
Brad, Calvin, 2
Bridging, 64
Brown, Sam, 2
Brown, Vic, 4

Calisthenics. *See* Floorwork.
Cheek protectors, 8
Chuvalo, George, 4
Clay, Cassius. *See* Muhammed Ali.
Clinch, 47
Clothing, 10
Combinations, 49-50, 62
Conditioning, 67-73
Cooper, Henry, 4
Corbett, 12
Counterpunching, 18, 47

Daniels, Terry, 4
Defense, 23, 41-47
   against left-handed boxer, 53
Diet, 72
Dipper, 65
Dundee, Angelo, 51
Durelle, Yvon, 2

Ellis, Jimmy, 4
Equipment, 8-12
Eye focus, while boxing, 21

Fear, 51
Feinting, 37-39
Ferdinand, Esau, 2
Fighting out of a crouch, 18, 39
Fight record, 2-4
Floorwork, 64-65
Footwork, 19, 55
Foreman, George, 7, 29, 53, 62
Forte, Levi, 4
Frazier, Joe, 7, 39, 62
Fusari, Charlie, 69

Gannon, Joe, 2
Gavilan, Kid, 50
Gazelle Punch, 50
Gloves, 11, 58
Gobold, Eddie, 2
Golden Gloves, 7, 67
Graham, Billy, 69
Grant, Don, 2
Green, Charlie, 4
Griffin, Jules, 50

Hand
Hands, care of, 12-15
Harris, Charlie, 4
Harris, Roy, 3
Harrison, Tommy, 2
Headguard, 8
Health rules, 72-73
Heavy bag, 11, 61-63
Herring, Tod, 4
Hitting and holding, 35

Infighting, 32, 35-37
Isometric exercise, 68-69

Jab, 25, 25-28
Jackson, Lester, 2
Jackson, Tommy "Hurricane," 3

Jeffries, James J., 38
Jogging, 69
Johansson, Ingemar, 3, 25, 32, 50
Johnson, Willie, 4

Lavelle, Frank, 50
Left-handed boxers, 25, 28, 51-53
Left hook, 25, 30-32
Light bag. *See* Speed bag.
Liston, Sonny, 3, 51, 62
London, Brian, 3

Machen, Eddie, 3, 25
Marciano, Rocky, 35, 41
Massage, 65
Maxim, Joey, 2
McBride, Archie, 2
McMurray, Bill, 4
McNeeley, Tom, 3
Medicine ball, 65
Mental attitude, 73
Mieszala, Chester, 2
Moore, Archie, 3, 28, 39, 41, 45, 50, 65
Mouthpiece, 8
Muldoon, Bill, 12
Muscle development, 68-69
  for hands, 15

Offense, 23, 25-39
  against left-handed boxer, 53
One-two combination, 34

Parrying, 41
Pastrano, Willie, 12
Peek-a-boo defense, 45
Pep, Willie, 47
Polite, Charlie, 4
Position of body
  in basic stance, 17-19
  in infighting, 35
Powell, Charley, 3
Practice
  for bobbing and weaving, 23
  for infighting, 35
  for jab, 28
Protective cup, 8
Protective equipment, 8-10
Punching, 58-62
Punching bags, 11-12
Punching out of a weave, 23
Push-ups, 65

Quarry, Jerry, 4

Rademacher, Peter, 3
Right cross, 25, 34-35
Right hook, 25, 28-29
Ring, 8
Roadwork, 69-72
Robe, 10
Robinson, Sugar Ray, 69
Rope-skipping, 62
Royer-Crecy, Jacques, 2
Rules, 8
Russell, Roger, 4

Sabotin, Lalu, 2
Sabotin, Lalu, 2
Saddler, Sandy, 28
Safetyin care of hands, 12-15
  in lifting weights, 68
    See also Protective equipment.
Shadow boxing, 55-56
"Shakedown cruise," 55
Sit-ups, 64
Skip ropes, 11
Slade, Jimmy, 2
Sliding, 17
Slipping punches, 20-21, 41-44
Sluggers, 49
Southpaws. See Left-handed boxers.
Sparring, 8, 56
Speed bag, 11, 58-61
Stance, 17-19
Sting Like a Bee, 39
Strategy, 49-53
Sullivan, 12
Sweat suits, 10

Torres, Jose, 12, 37
Training equipment, 11-12
Tray, Willie, 2
Trunks, 10
Turner, Jesse, 2

Uppercut, 25, 32-34

Wagner, Dick, 2
Walker, Sammy, 2
Wallace, Gordon, 2
Walls, Jimmy, 2
Weight control, 10, 65, 72
Weightlifting, 68
Where to learn boxing, 7-8
Whitlock, Dave, 2
Williams, Alvin, 2
Workouts, 55-65